Designed by Patricia Mitter

Library of Congress Cataloging-in-Publication
Data available.

ISBN: 978-1-943645-23-7

Manufactured in China

10 9 8 7 6 5 4 3 2 1

Produced by the Cornell Lab Publishing Group
120A North Salem Street
Apex, NC 27502

www.CornellLabPG.com

MIX
Paper from
responsible sources
FSC® C124385

CPSIA tracking label information
Production Location: Everbest Printing,
Guangdong, China
Production Date: 12/15/2017
Cohort: Batch No. 80307

By buying products with the FSC label you are supporting the growth
of responsible forest management worldwide.

An Eagle's Feather

BASED ON A STORY BY THE PHILIPPINE EAGLE FOUNDATION

By Minfong Ho

Illustrations by Frances Alvarez

TheCornellLab Publishing Group

Flying high above the forest
of Tambala at sunrise, Kalayaan
spots a monkey. Food!

The young Philippine eagle swoops down to follow the monkey.

Where did it go?

On and on Kalayaan flies in pursuit of it. He notices the landscape below changing.

Where are the trees? Where are the animals? Who are those people?

Scared, he turns to fly back when
BOOM! There is a shotgun blast, and
a sharp pain in his wing! In a flurry of
feathers and blood, he starts to fall,
and keeps falling.

Kalayaan crashes onto the hard ground.
He is dazed and weak, unable to get up.
Suddenly he hears footsteps and voices
approaching. What is happening?

"He's been shot, father!"
Kalayaan hears a boy's voice
shouting. "Must be a hunter
nearby. Hurry!"

Kalayaan feels the gentle
touch of small hands, and big,
strong arms wrapping him
in a cloth, and carrying him.
Then everything turns dark.

When he wakes up, Kalayaan
does not know where he is.
Instead of trees, there are metal
bars all around him. He tries to fly
but his hurt wing is bound tight.

And who's that in the other
corner of his cage?
Another...eagle?

"What is this place?" Kalayaan asks.

"Why are we here?"

"We are safe here," says the other eagle.

"You were brought here by kind
villagers after you were shot by
hunters. My name is Pinpin,
and unlike you, I was born
and raised right here."

"But why would people want to shoot us? Do they dislike us?"

"No, in fact there was a time people thought of us as kings of the sky, because we were the strongest birds in the whole of the Philippines," Pinpin pauses, "but that was a long time ago."

Over the next few months, as
Kalayaan's wing heals, the two
eagles spend their time getting
to know each other more.

Pinpin talks of how, according to what her mother told her, the forest has been cut down for timber, so that eagles have less and less space to hunt for food. "That's when people started hunting us down," Pinpin says, "and there are not many of us left now."

"So we are kept in these cages for our own safety," Kalayaan asks, "and I will never see my forest home again?"

"Don't lose hope," Pinpin comforts her new friend. "Someday we may both be set free into the forest, just like my mother was."

"She told me to live for that day, when
I grew big enough to be released. And
after that, I could find a mate and build
a nest to raise baby eagles in safety."

"And me?" Kalayaan asks.
"Will I be set free again, too?"
"I hope so," Pinpin says.

The two eagles stare at the
bars of their cage as the
leaves of the forests beyond
shimmer in the moonlight.

One day, after a very long time, Kalayaan and Pinpin wake up to a quiet morning. The day of their release back into the wild has finally come.

They are wrapped in cloth and taken to
the forest, and at first light, they are set
free. Kalayaan and Pinpin are so excited!

One, two, three, and off they fly!

Back in the forest of Tambala, there is no cage. There are no wounds on their wings.

The air is fresh, and they feel so happy to see the lush forest and the boundless blue sky.

"It's so beautiful out here, just like in mother's stories," Pinpin says. "Everything feels so new, but it is so good to fly free!"

"This is where we belong, Pinpin," Kalayaan replies. "At last, we are home!"

From the branches and leaves,
they hear a familiar voice.

"It's them!" says the boy.
"Hurry, father!" They wave up
to the eagles, smiling.

Kalayaan swoops down and flaps his wings to thank them, and continues to fly off with Pinpin into the dawn.

Learn more about the Great Philippine Eagle

Photo by Neil Rettig

Photo by Kike Arnal

The Philippine eagle has special feathers around its neck. An eagle might make its feathers stand up or lie down, depending on its mood. They might spread out their feathers to show they are paying attention, or to look bigger, or to help them hear sounds better, like when you cup your hands behind your ears.

Watch out monkeys, flying lemurs, and giant cloud rats—there is an eagle soaring over your forest home, and it is looking for food! This eagle is found only in the Philippines, a country of more than 7,600 islands in the Pacific Ocean. It lives in tropical mountain forests on just four of these islands: Mindanao, Luzon, Samar, and Leyte.

The Great Philippine Eagle is a giant in the eagle family. It stands more than three feet tall and can weigh more than 13 pounds. It has unusual pale gray eyes, a very large and deep blue-gray beak, huge black talons, and long feathered legs to carry off its large prey.

Photo by Neil Rettig

The Philippine eagle is a skilled flyer. Even though it is one of the largest and heaviest eagles in the world, it can fly in dense tropical forests without hitting any branches or trees.

Photo by Kike Arnal

Great Philippine Eagles like to use the tallest tree around for their nest, so they have a good view over their forest. The parents take turns feeding the chick and shielding it from the sun.

Photo by Neil Rettig

An eagle chick must grow for about five months before it leaves the nest. Even after it leaves, the young bird cannot kill its own prey until it is almost a year old. Its parents will continue to bring it food for almost two years.

These eagles mate for life, and take turns incubating their eggs. Once the chicks hatch, the couple spends a lot of time taking care of their chicks. Sometimes they even hunt together, with one bird distracting the prey while the other swoops in to grab it. A pair of eagles needs as much as 50 square miles of tropical forest for hunting so they can find enough food for themselves and their young.

Sadly, the Great Philippine Eagle is one of the rarest birds in the world.

Saving the Eagles

PHILIPPINE EAGLE
FOUNDATION

The Great Philippine Eagle is the national bird of the Philippines, but it is critically endangered. Only about 400 are left in the wild. For 30 years, the Philippine Eagle Foundation has been fighting hard to protect Philippine eagles from extinction.

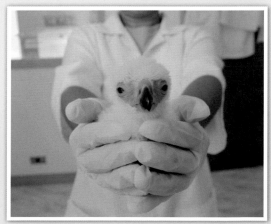

Photo by Eric Liner

A newly hatched Philippine eagle chick at the Philippine Eagle Foundation.

Photo by Eric Liner

A tiny eagle chick is growing inside this egg. Tinuy-an is the mother eagle who was named after a famous waterfall in the Philippines.

Every year, at least one Philippine eagle is killed because of shooting, even though there are laws to protect them. The Philippine Eagle Foundation helps people learn about these beautiful birds so that more people will appreciate and not hurt them. If the foundation finds any injured birds, they try to help them recover and release them back to the wild.

Protecting the forest is also very important for Great Philippine Eagles. Without forests, the eagles cannot survive. The Philippine Eagle Foundation helps people understand the importance of the forest, not only for the eagles but for the many plants and animals that live there.

The foundation works with villages to help protect the eagles. Every time a villager reports the location of a nest, the foundation will pay them, and the whole village, too. This information helps the foundation with their research and the money improves the lives of people in the village.

The foundation also finds out what the villages need, such as a water system or a school building, and they may even provide fertilizer so a village will reuse land rather than cutting down the forest for farmland.

Eagles Up Close

Photo by Kike Arnal

This man works with Great Philippine Eagles to help them breed. He wears a thick leather jacket, gloves, and hood so he won't get hurt by the bird's huge talons and powerful, sharp beak.

Philippine eagles that will no longer survive in the wild are kept at the foundation. Their caretakers wear thick leather jackets and gloves at all times to protect themselves from the birds' powerful talons. They help them breed in captivity so that young eagles can be released into the wild someday. Visitors enjoy seeing these amazing birds up close.

Download **BIRD QR** free on the iTunes or Android store.

Listen!

Scan this symbol with BIRD QR to hear what the Great Philippine Eagle sounds like!

Watch!

Scan this symbol with BIRD QR to watch *Kalayaan*, a children's film about the Great Philippine Eagle!

Learn More!

Scan this symbol with BIRD QR to learn more about the Great Philippine Eagle on the All About Birds website, *AllAboutBirds.org*.

Help the Great Philippine Eagle

Scan this symbol with BIRD QR to find out how you can support the Philippine Eagle Foundation. Or visit their website at: *PhilippineEagleFoundation.org*

The Cornell Lab of Ornithology is a nonprofit organization dedicated to the study, appreciation, and conservation of birds.

A portion of the sales of *An Eagle's Feather* will go directly to the Philippine Eagle Foundation which is fighting hard to protect the Great Philippine Eagle from extinction.

The**Cornell**Lab of Ornithology